GW01179402

FIRST TECHNOLOGY

Tools

Author: **John Williams**
Photographer: **Zul Mukhida**

You will need . . .

A grater, a tin, a rolling-pin,
A sieve, a bowl to stir it in,
Some paper to grease around the grooves,
A knife to make it nice and smooth.
A spoon to stir, a rack to cool,
A pretty, star-shaped cutting tool.

Does it really have to take
All these things to bake a cake?

Wayland

FIRST TECHNOLOGY

Titles in this series

Energy

Machines

Tools

Wheels and Cogs

WARNING: Tools can be dangerous and must always be handled with care. Young children should always be supervised when using tools.

First published in 1993 by
Wayland (Publishers) Ltd
61 Western Road, Hove
East Sussex BN3 1JD, England

British Library Cataloguing in Publication Data

Williams, John
Tools – (First Technology Series)
I. Title II. Series
621.9

ISBN 0 7502 0650 0

Typeset by DJS Fotoset Ltd, Brighton, Sussex.
Printed and bound in Turin, Italy, by Canale.

Series editor: Kathryn Smith
Designer: Loraine Hayes
Photos organized by Zoë Hargreaves

Poem by Catherine Baxter.

Words printed in **bold** appear in the glossary on page 31.

HELIX

Look at your hands. How many fingers and thumbs do you have? There are many things we can do with our hands.
We can do up buttons . . .
. . . open cans of drink.

Our hands cannot do everything. Sometimes we need to use **tools**.

We can use tools to hammer . . .

. . . to clean

. . . to cut

We use tools everyday . . .

. . . at home

. . . at work

. . . at school

We use a knife, fork and spoon to eat.

We use a pencil to write.

We use a spade to dig.

Which tools have you used today?

Tools are safe if you use them properly.

Some tools can pinch.

Some tools are very heavy.

Some tools have sharp points.

Some tools have sharp edges.

Always hold the tool in the right way. Never run when you are holding a tool.

Each tool has a special **job**.
These tools are used to mend a **puncture**.

A carpenter uses these tools to make wooden **furniture**.

These children are making biscuits. Which tools are they using?

Who would use these tools?

A doctor uses special tools at work.

Where would you find these tools?
LEIFHEIT

To do a job well,
we need to use
the best tool for
the job.
Would you use
a garden fork to
eat spaghetti?

Which of these drills does your dentist use?

A tool has to be the right size for a job. Some jobs are very small. We need to use very small tools.

Some jobs are big.
We need to use large tools.

Can you match these tools to the right job?

Plant
Screws
Bare chest
Dirty finger nails

These children are using tools to do different jobs. How many tools can you spot?

Can you find these tools?
Pliers
Hammer
Ruler

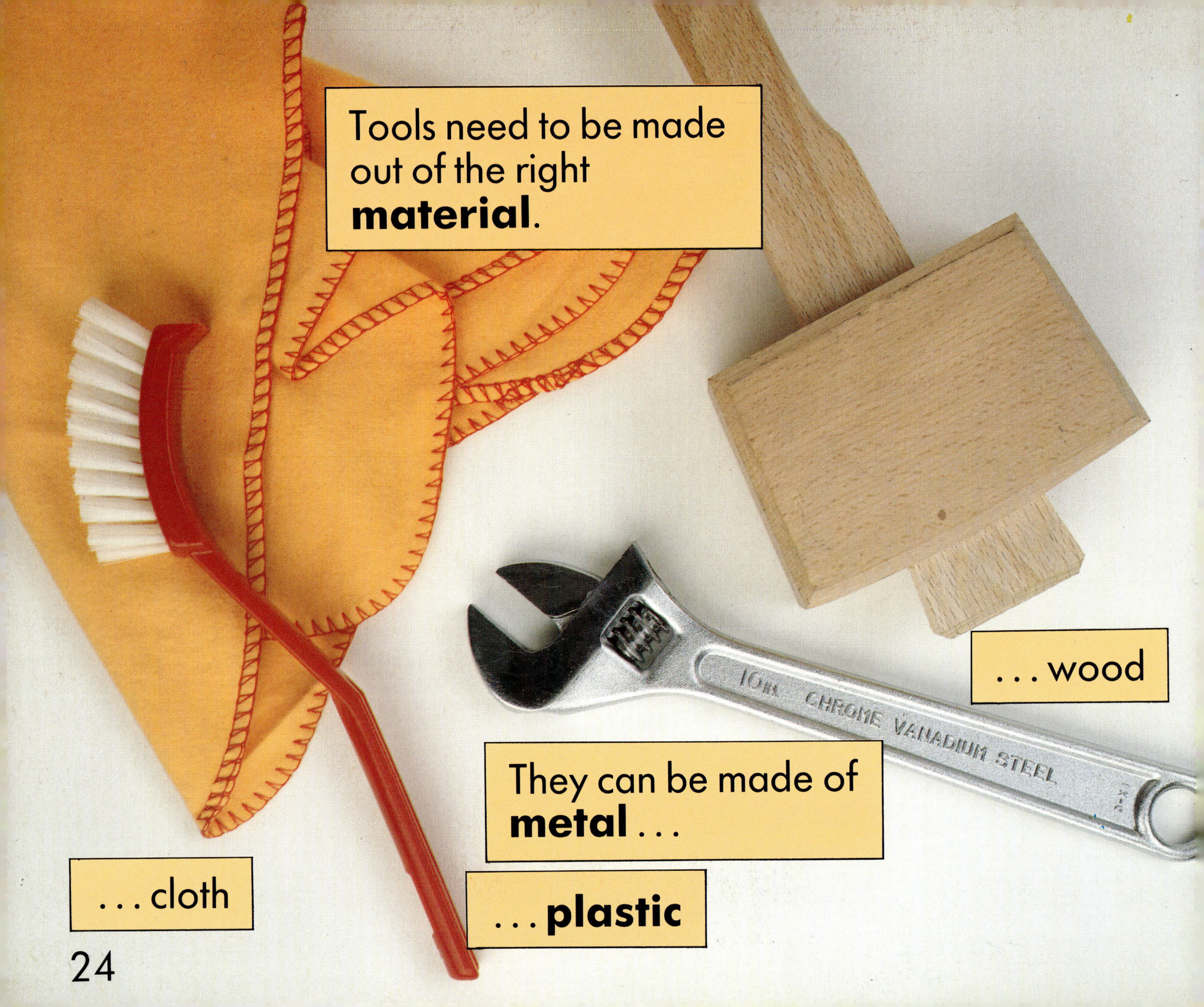

Tools need to be made out of the right **material**.

They can be made of **metal** . . .

. . . wood

. . . cloth

. . . **plastic**

A tea towel must be able to soak up water to dry wet dishes.
A pan scrubber must be scratchy to clean dirty pans.

A hammer must be hard and heavy, to bang in nails.

What would happen if a tool was made from the wrong material?

What is wrong with these buckets?

Using tools to make a paper streamer

You will need a 30 cm strip of 1 cm square section wooden dowel rod, some coloured tissue paper and glue.
Look at these pictures and make a list of the tools you will need.
Will you need to use any tools more than once?

1. **Measure** a piece of dowel 30 cm long, and mark it with a pencil.

2. Put the dowel in a vice and use a junior hack-saw to cut it to length.

3. Cut ten strips of tissue paper.

4. Use some glue to stick the tissue paper on to the rod.

NOTES FOR TEACHERS AND PARENTS

Children need to learn to use tools at an early age, to aid the development of their manipulative skills. Under close supervision, they should be allowed to investigate the properties and purposes of a wide variety of tools. These should include familiar objects which children might not regard as tools, such as writing and kitchen equipment, as well as saws, hand drills, hammers, and screwdrivers. Good safety practices must be followed at all times.

Children should also be encouraged to discover more about the groups of tools used in the adult world, for example those used by dentists, mechanics, builders and artists.

Simple tools which can be used safely and effectively in the classroom are available from many suppliers. These tools include:

Saws A junior hack-saw is the best for this age group. When using them, the wood should be securely held in a vice or a bench hook.

Hammers These should be small and light, with a firm grip.

Screwdrivers These can be used to connect bulbs and batteries. A 'phillips' screwdriver will be needed if the screw has a cross-shaped groove.

Pliers These can be used for holding screws, bolts or nuts in place while they are being adjusted.

Drills Small hand drills are quite safe for use by young children. Adults will need to help children change the drill-bits, and understand how the drill chuck holds them in place.

Scissors Some scissors are specially designed for use by young children. They cut well, but have no sharp points. They often have coloured plastic handles which indicate left- or right-handed use.

Using tools

The streamer activity is included to enable children to use some of the tools covered in this book, and has been tested in the classroom in both infant and nursery schools.

Before they start building, the children should be encouraged to decide which tools they will need. They can sort the tools out into the order they will be used. This skill will help them to understand, and to cope with the design and testing processes to which they will be introduced at a later stage. The children should be encouraged to try to measure accurately, although at this young age, there is no need to place too much emphasis on this.

GLOSSARY

Furniture Chairs, tables, beds, and other things like this that belong in the house.

Job Work to be done.

Material Something like cloth, metal, plastic or wood, which is made into things.

Measure Find out how long, heavy or big an object is.

Metal A hard, often shiny material, which first has to be dug from the ground.

Plastic A special material which is strong, but not very heavy.

Pliers A small tool used to bend wire.

Puncture A small hole in a tyre.

Stethoscope A tool used by a doctor to listen to your heartbeat or breathing.

Tools Things that are held in the hand, and have been made to do special jobs.

Vice A tool for holding something tightly in place. When you cut wood, you should always hold it in a vice.

INDEX